Stars, Planets, Nebulae, and Black Holes

Children's Science & Nature

BABY PROFESSOR

EDUCATION KIDS

Speedy Publishing LLC
40 E. Main St. #1156
Newark, DE 19711
www.speedypublishing.com

How big is our galaxy? Have you ever looked up at the starry skies at night and wondered how far away they are? The enchanting skies tell us how magnificent and mysterious the universe is.

Let's explore the galaxy and learn interesting facts about stars, planets, nebulae and black holes. Billions and Billions of Stars! Stars are bright cosmic energy engines everywhere in the universe. Our sun is a star. Stars are made up of gas and plasma, and hot matter composed of subatomic particles.

Did you know that most stars are bigger than the sun? Stars are very big, and most of them are even brighter than the sun.

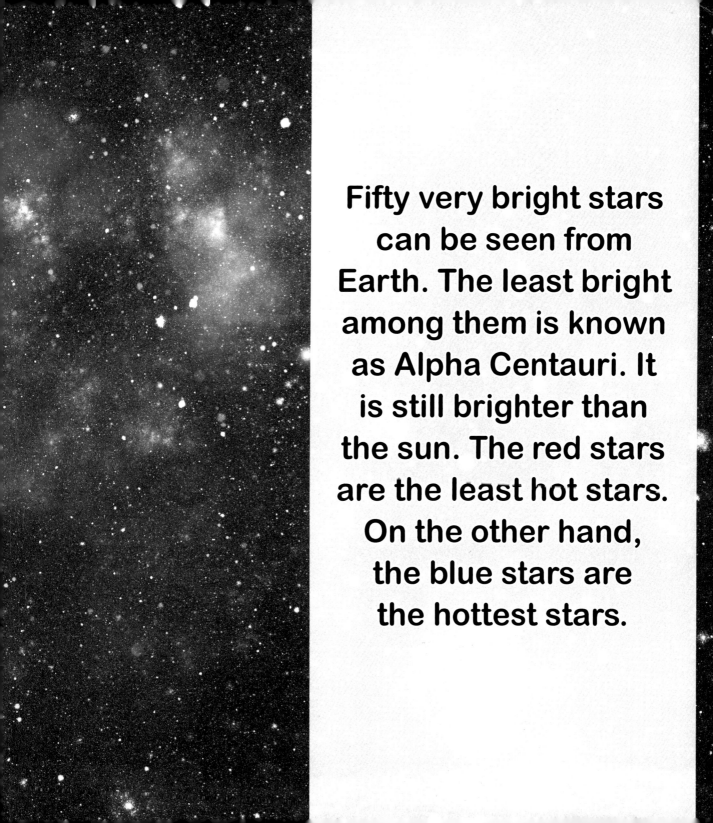

Fifty very bright stars can be seen from Earth. The least bright among them is known as Alpha Centauri. It is still brighter than the sun. The red stars are the least hot stars. On the other hand, the blue stars are the hottest stars.

Did you know that stars are black bodies? These black- colored objects absorbs light, radio waves and all other electromagnetic radiation. Interestingly, stars radiate back all they have absorbed and even more. Amazingly, stars are black bodies that shine with deep brilliance.

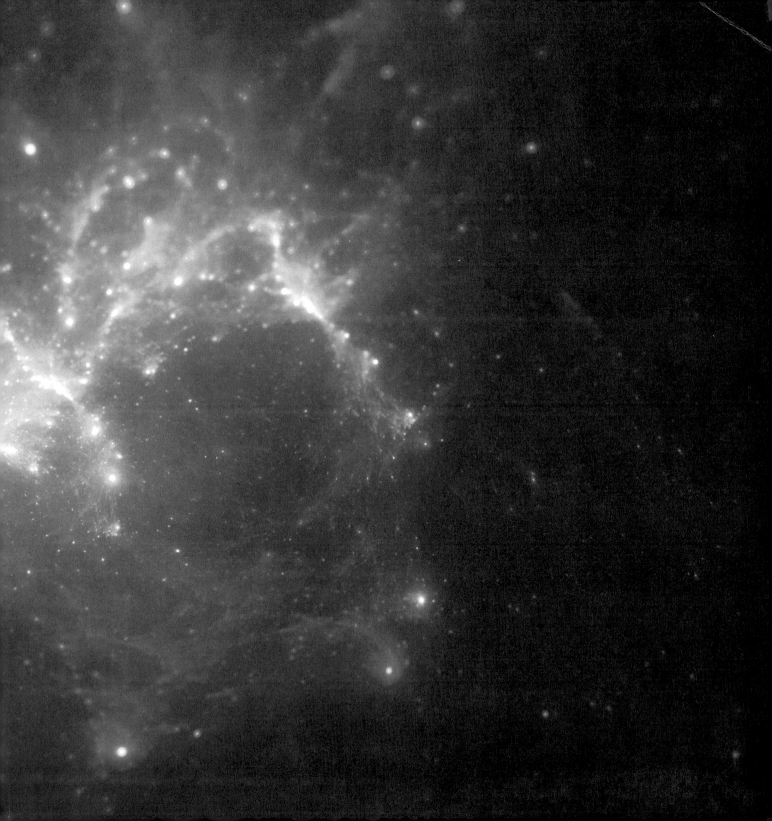

Old-aged stars are referred to as giants and supergiants. The majority of stars are in their mature stage and are called dwarfs. Our sun is a dwarf star.

Do stars twinkle? This is very interesting. Stars don't twinkle or scintillate. But why do they appear twinkling? That is why we sing twinkle, twinkle little star. The twinkling that we see is caused by the earth's turbulent atmosphere.

Just how cool is
the Universe?
Let's talk about the
amazing planets in
our solar system!

We live on just one planet, and the others fascinate us. Planets are some of the objects that orbit around the sun due to its gravity. Along with the planets are the comets, asteroids, and moons.

There are eight beautiful planets in our solar system. Four of them are closer to the sun. These are Mercury, Venus, Earth and Mars. They are known as terrestrial planets or the inner planets. These planets appeared to be smaller and are mostly made of rock and metal.

The four outer planets are Jupiter, Saturn, Uranus and Neptune. These planets are known as gas giants. They are much larger than the terrestrial planets. They are mainly made up of hydrogen, helium and other gases.

Scientists have discovered five dwarf planets in the solar system. These include Pluto, Ceres, Eris, Makemake and Haumea. There are many others, deeper in our solar system, waiting to be discovered.

What are Nebulae? The word comes from the Latin word Nebula, which means cloud. Nebulae are clouds between the stars. These clouds are made up of plasma, helium, hydrogen and dust. They are not like clouds we see on Earth. They are not made up of water vapor.

Nebulae are extremely large. Some stretch across hundreds of light years. A light year is the distance that light travels in one year. It is almost impossible to imagine the size of just one nebula.

These interstellar clouds are formed by the gravitational breakdown of gases. When particles collapse, they clump together because of their gravity. This is how nebulae are formed.

Did you know that stars are usually formed inside nebulae? Hence, nebulae are known as the star nurseries.

Interestingly, nebulae have thousands of different shapes. They look like crabs, butterflies, horse heads and many more shapes.

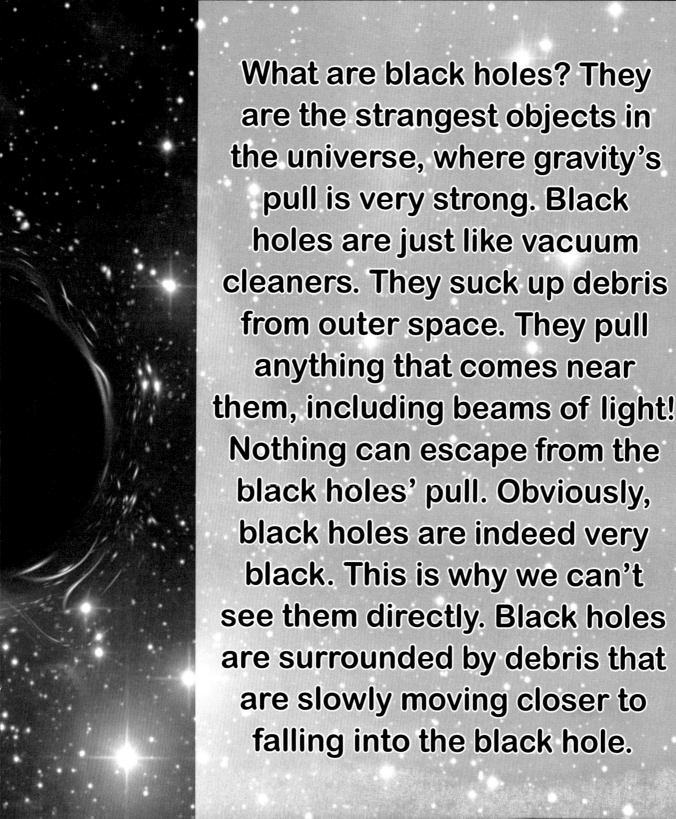

What are black holes? They are the strangest objects in the universe, where gravity's pull is very strong. Black holes are just like vacuum cleaners. They suck up debris from outer space. They pull anything that comes near them, including beams of light! Nothing can escape from the black holes' pull. Obviously, black holes are indeed very black. This is why we can't see them directly. Black holes are surrounded by debris that are slowly moving closer to falling into the black hole.

Black holes are composed of three main parts. The outer layer is called the Outer Event Horizon. The middle layer is known as the Inner Event Horizon. The center of the black hole is the Singularity. It has the strongest gravity pull. A black hole has no surface.

There is more to know about the stars, planets, nebulae and black holes. Research and have fun!

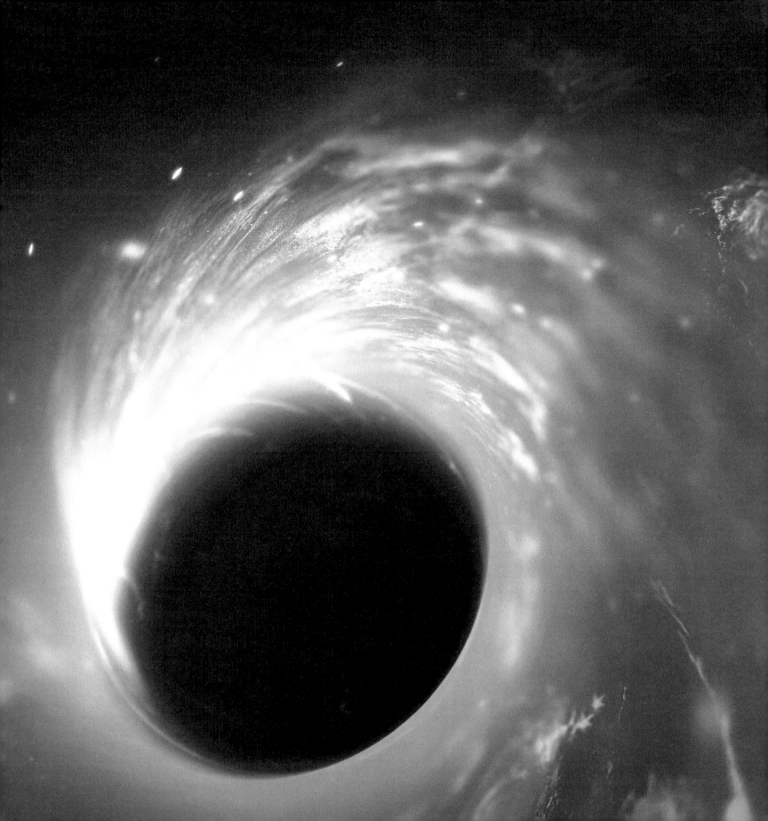

Visit

BABY PROFESSOR
EDUCATION KIDS

www.BabyProfessorBooks.com

to download Free Baby Professor eBooks
and view our catalog of new and exciting
Children's Books

Made in the USA
Lexington, KY
21 November 2018